Introduction

+++++++++++++++++++++++++++++++++++++++

In This Part

- ➢ What do you get from this book?
- ➢ Importance of Credit

++

You are no stranger to credit. But when it comes to Business Credit, the fascination isn't there. You want to start a business, buy inventory, sell products, market and advertise your products and services, so on and so on. However, you just don't get it and it's not your fault.

You see, owing and managing a small business is fun and exciting. Small business entrepreneurs believe that managing their business is involving. It's not an easy task! This is because small businesses face some sort of problems in the course of their lifetime.

Thousands of small businesses start every year throughout the world and the chances of survival depends solely on credit. In order to create a stable business, you will need access to credit from time to time. Starting a business is one thing, but running it you will need open access to corporate or business credit.

What do you get from this book?

That's where this book comes in handy. Instead of getting worked up and driving your personal credit in business, it will enlighten you on corporate credit and how it works. It's a high time we changed our mindset on the conventional and traditional myths of using personal credit to getting started in business.

There is a difference between personal credit and corporate credit. Personal credit is for personal use whereas corporate credit is for running businesses. What personal credit will do is limited as opposed to corporate credit that will scale your investments and open new windows of opportunities. Personal credit is built upon spending habits which you must watch out. But corporate credit is built with trade relations that you do business with. Watch out mixing the two credit issues together because they will ruin your life. You will be able to do that and more by reading through the simple step-by-step instruction and solve the mystery of corporate credit. The business world views credit differently. If you are in business as a solo entrepreneur and have no plans to hire employees or form some partnership, you may not see the need to use corporate credit. However, I will still recommend the use of corporate credit in order to counter cash flow needs that may arise.

Importance of Credit

Most of us at some point will need credit. The importance of borrowing is to extend a lifeline to your cash flow, be it personal or business. Whether you are starting a business, purchased a business, experiencing cash flow problems or building a business, you will need corporate credit. Understanding this term 'credit' is crucial before proceeding to borrow.

Contents at a Glance

Introduction...2

> What do you get from this book?.................................3
> Importance of Credit..3

Part 1: Revealing Credit...................................4

> What is Credit?..4
> Understanding Personal and Corporate Credit.............5
> Why You Need Corporate Credit................................6

Part 2: Corporate Credit Building Checklist..........7

> Business legal name...8
> Incorporation...9
> Business address & Telephone Number......................10
> Applying For an EIN Number......................................11
> Open a business account...12
> Registering with credit corporate firms.....................13

Part 3: Establishing and Building Corporate Credit For your Business.......................................14

> Who is Dun & Bradstreet?...15
> Start listing Your Trade References with DNB.............17
> Applying for your Corporate credit............................19
> How to invest in you and your business.....................22

Part 4: How to apply for credit cards...................23

> Getting Credit Limits on your cards............................23
> Factors to look for when selecting a credit card..........24
> Secure and unsecured business credit cards...............26

++

Notes Section:

Part 1

Revealing Credit

++

- ➢ What is Credit?
- ➢ Understanding Personal and Corporate Credit
- ➢ Why You Need Corporate Credit

++

This part introduces you to credit, and the importance of using credit in your business.

What is Credit?

We all have worked with credit at some point. If so, let's replay the scenario here because credit starts from scratch. Some people too often run into personal credit as a lifesaver without understanding the terms and knowing the conditions of repayment. Well, corporate credit is different from personal credit because it comes with different perks that are hinged on your purpose of borrowing.

So, what is credit?

You see, you are the definition of the word 'credit' before it translates to monetary value. Whether it is personal or corporate credit, you are the face of the transaction. Your proven track record in repaying and the bill of health of your personal or business finances speak on your behalf. This is what lenders call in business, credit worthiness.

Understanding Personal and Corporate Credit

Because many people use personal credit does not mean that they understand credit. From secured credit cards to unsecured credit cards, some people have failed in their responsibilities to repay even the minimum credit amounts offered to them. Let's say you have acquired an unsecured personal credit card and drained it all in one shopping spree in the mall. You will need to pay up the balance incurred in your personal credit card regardless of your financial situation. Personal credit is for personal use only where you use and pay back with your income. Whether you are employed or running a business, you will need to pay up your dues on time. Failure to pay on time will end up hurting your credit rating plunging to low credit scores and destroying your credit worthiness.

Corporate credit is the money accessed from credit lenders to run and manage your business operations on a day-to-day basis. This performance-based cash lending is provided after you satisfy the terms and conditions of the corporate credit lender. They will analyze the volume of cash flow in your business, which is a better indicator of your company's financial health than your personal credit score. Remember corporate credit is scored differently because it involves large amounts of money as opposed to personal credit that start you of small amounts. Depending on what stage of your business is in, whether you are starting or building, evaluating your proposal is critical in order to develop an idea on where to go for corporate credit assistance.

Why you need Corporate Credit

The benefits of using corporate credit are numerous compared to using personal credit. Businesses that use corporate credit usually have longevity and record success. Corporate lenders understand the challenges of building a business through equity, debt and off-balance sheet financing, maintaining cash flow, making payroll, business expansion and inventory/equipment management. Here are other benefits:

- ➢ Separate and differentiate business from personal expenses
- ➢ Cushion your business from cash flow problems
- ➢ Build the business brand to have its own entity
- ➢ Equip the business by purchasing necessary tools and equipment
- ➢ Build equity in order to attract potential investors
- ➢ Open trade lines with vendors and manufacturers
- ➢ Maintain cash flow for your business operations
- ➢ Develop both your personal and business status

Part 2

Things You'll Need for Corporate Credit

+++

In This Part

- ➤ Finding a business name
- ➤ Registering the business name
- ➤ Using a business address & telephone number for contact
- ➤ Applying for an EIN Number
- ➤ Registering with credit reporting firms
- ➤ Opening a bank account
- ➤ Building your corporate credit
- ➤ Applying for your 1st corporate credit
- ➤ How to invest in you and your business

+++

Now that we have established the difference between personal and corporate credit, we will now discuss the next important step of how to build corporate credit using your startup business. We will follow the list above as a step-by-step for you to understand and establishing credit worthiness using your business. Remember, I am trying to dissuade you from using your personal credit and work using this business approach. This is methodical; therefore, follow the directions sequentially to the last and you will find success in your 1st corporate credit application.

This is your personal book; therefore, follow the steps listed and make notes on each section to help focus and be able to identify them later on how you worked through to building your 1st business credit.

Step 1: Finding a legal business name

Find a unique name that reflects your business model, product or service offered that is different from other(s) in the competition. The problem is not coming up with a business name but one that is acceptable by your state during registration. Places to do a name search are Dun & Bradstreet (DNB), your city municipal office or local state commission office websites. The purpose of doing a name search is to find out if there is another business using the name you want for your business. If there is not, then the name is yours and good to go. Never and never use an existing name found in the databases.

Point to note: Dun & Bradstreet (DNB) is a business credit reporting agency with over 100 million businesses registered in their database. Since they collect and keep record of business credit reports, you will be able to confirm that the business name you are searching for is available before proceeding to doing a search with your local municipal or state office. DNB are credible and this is where you will go after you register your company name and get an EIN Number.

++

Notes Section:

Step 2: Registering the business name

This is a must-do step in order to get your business legal and accepted for credit. Decide your business structure whether it will be C-Corporation, S-Corporation, Sole Proprietorship or LLC-Limited Liability Company. For the purpose of separating personal credit from business credit, LLC or C-Corporation is a great way to structure the business. You will file for registration with your state local commission office. There is a fee, check with your city and local state offices for this service. Also, you can use online registration companies or hire a business attorney for this service.

++

Notes Section:

Step 3: Using a business address & Telephone Number for contact

If you are a business start-up, using your home physical address is fine as you start your business. Eventually, you will grow and seek some office or warehouse space in order to appeal and look professional. However, using a business physical address is a great start if you have one. You must provide a proper address where you can be reached. It has to be a valid physical address. Also, provide a valid email address and telephone number. It's good practice to have an address associated with your business name and a local area code telephone number where you are running the business. Never use a different area code telephone number outside your location.

+++

Notes Section:

Step 4: Applying for an EIN Number

For any registered company to operate business legally, you will need to apply for an Employer Identification Number (EIN.) This Tax ID number is part of what the lenders want together with your registered name and business address to be identified as a legal business entity. Applying for this number is FREE and fast. As a sole proprietor or business owner, you simply go to www.irs.gov

+++

Notes Section:

Step 5: Open A Business Account

This may sound too early but the advantage of it is in Step 7. The reason I suggest opening an account now is that you are aligning yourself with a business reference. You can choose your local bank or a community credit union bank and open with the minimum opening balance they suggest to you. The advantages of a local credit union bank is that they are a safe place to save and borrow at reasonable rates with good returns on interest rates. If you are intending to buy a house or property down the road, credit union banking is your new best friend.

Also, while at it, try and see if you can open a secured business credit card. The game here is aligning with your bank and starting to build a business relationship.

+++

Notes Section:

Step 6: Registering with Credit Reporting Firms

This is an area I call the 'missing link' because it's the most crucial piece of information that you will need in order to apply for corporate credit. You will need to register and establish a business credit profile with credit reporting firms who will record your activities with your business contacts and/or supplier(s.) Why is this step important, you may ask? Here is why…Just like your personal credit that is reported to TransUnion, Equifax and Experian, business credit is also reported similarly but with different agencies. In business credit reporting, these credit bureaus collect data from banks, suppliers, finance companies, business owners, and look at public records such as tax liens, bankruptcies, and judgments.

+++

Notes Section:

Part 3

Establishing and Building Corporate Credit For Your Business

+++

In This Part

> ➢ Registering with credit reporting firms
> ➢ Who is Dun & Bradstreet?
> ➢ Building your corporate credit profile
> ➢ Applying for your 1st corporate credit
> ➢ Checklist
> ➢ How to invest in you and your business

+++

It's important for you to get your company listed because it can make the process of establishing business credit and financing much easier. There are over 25 other **business credit bureaus** and some are industry specific such as construction and transportation. Here are the Top 10 Business Credit Bureaus you should know.

1. Dun and Bradstreet (DNB)
2. Equifax Small Business Enterprise
3. Experian SmartBusinessReportsTM
4. ChexSystems
5. ClientChecker
6. Credit.net
7. Paynet
8. AccurintTMBusiness
9. Cortera
10. FDInsight™

Dun and Bradstreet (D&B)

In this step, we will study Dun & Bradstreet (DNB) since they are the primary business credit reporting agency with over 100 million businesses registered in their database. They are the largest in the country (USA) and very popular with corporate credit lenders. They are the most famous in business credit rating who collect and publish business profiles of different businesses through their proprietary system called DUNS that stands for Data Universal Numbering System. They assign a unique numeric identifier, referred to as a "DUNS Number" to a single business entity. The DUNS Number is a nine-digit that identifies your business just like EIN or Social Security Number. The DUNS Number is FREE of charge!

As a popular credit reporting agency, you will need to be registered with them. Its business credit builder program is a great way for business owners to add trade references to their file in a short period of time. Applying for a DUNS Number is easy and simple. It's free of charge and there are three ways to get it.

1. FREE Option: This is the longer route and I DO NOT recommend it. Even though it's free of charge, it will take almost 30-60 days to get it.
2. $49 Option: This paid service gets you the number within 5 days.
3. $229-$1700 Option: This price-varied option gives you a number within 5 business days of the application with added incentive perks to your advantage. I would recommend sacrificing $229 or more and get you started right away. The best one is the $329 that will include credit profile building and set you a credit score. If you have questions, its best to call DNB and an agent on the phone will help you determine the packages and decide on which one.

+++

Notes Section:

Step 7: Start Listing Your Trade References with Dun & Bradstreet

You do not want to waste time in applying for business corporate credit once you have your DUNS Number. Creating a business credit profile is an additional service that comes with your number. Dun & Bradstreet will help you create the business profile the same day you get your number. This is where you will enter your bank that you opened your business account with as I mentioned in Step 5.

Also, you can add business telephone carrier service in here. You will need office supplies, hardware supplies and so on. Then apply for these store cards under your business name and list them in your trade references. For those who like flying, flyer miles card is also a great card to secure with one of the airlines. Even gas station companies do have gas cards which are a must-have for drivers. All these and more will establish your business profile and corporate credit lenders will see that you are in business with them. Subscribe to a business magazine in your field of business. These are other good resources for your business and most of them use the 'Bill Me Later' which they will mail it to you. Not all business networks and clients report your credit performance with the business credit bureau, so you might want to investigate before submitting them as trade reference

With these few activities of five or more contacts, Dun & Bradstreet will create your business profile immediately by activating the account. Populate your account with the list of contacts that you have and that can be done the same day you get your number. Once you have your DUNS Number, you can now start applying for business corporate credit.

++

Notes Section:

Step 8: Apply for Corporate Credit

Once you have your DUNS Number and populated your business credit profile, you can now start applying for business corporate credit. Look up for the credit company telephone numbers online and call them. Apply for corporate credit by calling their 1-800 numbers using your business telephone number that is associated with your business. You will have to guarantee your new startup business credit with your personal credit as this is your 1st business credit card. But the credit you build from this corporate credit card will be for the business. The credit card you get to fund your business primarily depends on how good your individual credit score is since you are responsible for the card's use. Over time, you will not need to use your personal credit at all because your business will have proven itself creditworthy.

Point to note: It's important not to only concentrate on building business credit; you should also establish a personal credit recovery plan so you can rebuild your own personal credit rating. Either of these options should get you started on business credit.

1. **Secured Business Credit Card:** It's exactly like any other credit card, except that you place a security deposit upon opening it and get it back when closing if in good standing. Certainly you will need it if you have bad credit and various banks offer different requirements starting from $200. This option guarantees approval regardless of your credit history or income. A good history with the credit card is good so that the bank may extend your line of credit or offer you an unsecured card. Your local commercial banks, online banking institutions and business credit card companies can assist you with this application.

2. **U.S Small Business Administration (SBA):** SBA financial assistance programs are tailored made to facilitate corporate credit for you with their lending partners. Also, some banks offer unsecured revolving lines of credit backed by the SBA which helps business owners meet short-term and working capital. It is a great option for new businesses. SBA helps you identify your financial need by assisting you with business finance from a corporate credit lender, guarantee a bond, or assist you find startup capital.

3. **1st Time Business Credit Cards:** Some credit card companies have custom credit card options for small business. They are designed to give you purchasing power as your business grows while earning cash or airline miles, for regular use. Since it will be your 1st business credit card, they will tie it with your personal credit information. Your personal credit score should be good and in good standing. Well known commercial banks and business credit card companies like American Express, Capital One and Chase are good picks in this category.

Here is Your Checklist:

- ✓ Name search using DNB, your municipal office or local state commission office
- ✓ Incorporating your business name
- ✓ Using a business address and local telephone number
- ✓ Applying for an EIN Number
- ✓ Open a business account
- ✓ Register with credit reporting firms; in this case, Dun & Bradstreet.
- ✓ Start listing your trade references with Dun & Bradstreet
- ✓ Apply for corporate credit

++

Notes Section:

Step 9: How to Invest in You and Your Business

Building business credit takes a lot of work. When you start your business, your net worth is zero. But as you start paying your dues, you put your business on a success path. It takes time to reach your net worth but you will eventually end up wiping off all the debt. Aim for a business growth pattern that will set you to attaining financial success. Some practical tips to help you achieve the status:

- ➢ Reduce unnecessary expenses
- ➢ Always maintain a positive cash flow
- ➢ Enlarge your markets
- ➢ Push for higher sales and create capacity
- ➢ Aim for more profit
- ➢ Find ways to reduce production costs
- ➢ Repay your entire credit before end of term
- ➢ Always pay your loans on time
- ➢ Always pay your credit on time
- ➢ Find ways to improve your money management methods
- ➢ Never mix personal credit with business credit
- ➢ Create accountable plans like expense and medical accounts

+++

Notes Section:

Part 4

How to apply for credit cards

++

In This Part

> ➤ Getting Credit Limits on your cards
> ➤ Factors to look for when selecting a credit card
> ➤ Secure and unsecured business credit cards

++

Getting credit limits on your cards

You have secured your 1st business credit card or even a 2nd one. The world of business is now becoming real and every purchase is within reach. Before you start using credit cards, read and understand the conditions and terms associated with the credit card. Business credit cards are powerful tools hence they should be handled with care not to misuse. Another line of credit is unsecured and/or secured credit that I mentioned earlier. These are the simple ways of getting started in securing credit cards and growing your credit profile.

By now you have realized that most credit lenders are providing a credit limit from as low as $10,000 to as much as $20,000 upon satisfaction. If you want higher limits, then you have to submit additional documents like financial statements as well as tax filing documents. Most banks and credit lenders would want to approve you higher credit limits after one-year. Still, there are private lenders who can fund your business after 3 months.

Factors to look for when selecting a credit card

Here a few important things that you should consider in choosing a business credit card:

Costs & Annual fees: Different cards charge differently. Most annual fees range from $24.95 to S99.95, while others don't charge. Be careful because these fees often fail to be budgeted in your repayment dues and they can be hefty. If you are biased against annual fees, consider your pick of cards wisely.

Interest rates: Some credit companies introduce a low interest rate (APR) for a short period usually as an introductory then increase it later on like after three of six months. Also, these can blind you in your budgetary payments when the teaser is over and you failed to follow up on the adjustment. Cash advancements also carry higher interest rates. This may affect your business if you are not watchful.

Line of credit: As you get started using your 1st credit card for your business, remember that these interest rates are usually higher. Credit cards are for rotating and unforeseen expenses not for operating a business.

Incentive Perks: Most credit cards offer kickbacks in the form of rewards and gifts. These incentives include cash back, frequent flyer miles, free gas and gift purchases. Check with the respective credit card provider for these incentive programs and how to enroll in them.

Business Credit Reporting: Not all business credit card companies report your credit performance to business-credit reporting bureaus. However, some good business credit card companies do update your payment data with business credit reporting bureaus. This helps the business establish some creditworthiness.

All in all, choosing a credit card means a lot and one should be informed. Always study the fine print language to see their hidden terms and conditions.

++

Notes Section:

Secure and unsecured business credit cards

These options are best for startups, small businesses and poor business rating. If you are doing well in business, then an unsecured business credit card is good for you. By opting to go for a secured credit card, you can slowly rebuild your poor business credit by using the card in a cautious manner. Your local bank where you opened your business account is the best option since they know you by banking with them. Banks are known to report to the credit bureaus timely and favorably.

A secured credit card will need you to deposit some amount of money with the credit card lender. The lender will put this amount as deposit on your card. In this approach, all the money deposited will appear as line of credit. So, if you deposit $1,000 into your account, your credit line is $1,000.

Secured credit cards usually attract low interests rates but goes up in increment annually. Many people overlook them in business because they are concentrating on establishing their credit profile and rating. However, you will need to raise the money upfront for the deposit. The credit lenders are good at monitoring your spending habits and once you satisfy your business needs, you can always request them to change it to an unsecured credit card.

A few months will pass and other corporate credit lenders will start sending you unsecured credit offers. This is because your business credit profile is beginning to look great and are considering you for credit applications. Remember to ascertain your needs before signing up any of them. There are many financial lenders that will look at your business within 3-6 months of starting your business to start loaning you. Business loans are other different business tools for financing and are great for business growth.

Your Business Resource Tools:

Small Business Administration is a complete guide to starting and expanding your business. You'll find information on counseling, training, capital, contracting, disaster assistance, business advocacy, local directories and more. Visit: http://www.sba.gov

Ready to form an LLC? The Company Corporation have helped hundreds of thousands of small business owners incorporate, file a DBA or form a limited liability company (LLC) whether you are a home based, office based, e-commerce or online. Their services and resources also include Operating Agreement, filing of an Employer Identification Number (EIN) with the IRS, and more! Visit: www.incorporate.com

Sweating for a business idea or startup business plan and do not where to start? The small business market is bursting with ideas and ready to have you on board. This magazine is excellent for anything startup, business building and entrepreneurial skill building. Subscribe yours today at: http://www.inc.com

Starting a business? Experian Small Business offers advice and resources you need to start a small business. They are a comprehensive company providing services in business financing, protective measures and establishing corporate credit. Visit: http://www.experiangroup.com

++

Notes Section: